DUSK TILL DAWN

DUSK'S LAMENTATION AND DAWN'S RESURGENCE

AAROHI BHATTACHARYA

To my parents, for putting up with my endless poetry recitals and late-night writing sessions.

To my brother Aviral, for making the writing process a bit more bearable with his antics, and most importantly, for helping me design the cover and edit the images for the book.

To my English teachers, Miss Candida Maria Viegas and Miss Rohini Nautiyal, for nurturing my love for poetry and guiding me throughout.

To Convent of Jesus and Mary, Waverley, my alma matter, for fostering an environment where creativity can flourish.

To all my friends, for pretending to understand my metaphors and not laughing too hard.

And to the dreamers, for proving that we're not the only ones with our heads in the clouds.

Contents

Contents

Contents

Preface

"To see a world in a grain of sand
And heaven in a wild flower,
Hold infinity in the palm of your hand
And eternity in an hour."
-William Blake

Prologue

प्रज्ञानं ब्रह्म : चेतना ही ब्रह्म है

अहं ब्रह्मास्मि : मैं ब्रह्म हूँ

तत्त्वमसि : वह तुम हो

अयमात्मा ब्रह्म : यह आत्मा ही ब्रह्म है

Acknowledgements

Writing these poems has been an incredible journey for me. As Anne Frank had said, "Paper is more patient than people", Therefore, I poured my heart out on each page.

I aimed to capture the full spectrum of grim teenage emotions, and expressing them has been an unforgettable experience.

One thing that I must mention is that it's an artist's job to portray emotions which they might not have ever felt...

I would like to extend my deepest gratitude to my parents for their unwavering support.

I hope you have an insightful reading !

DUSK'S LAMENTATION

1. Fake a smile

I fight my inner voice, put on a face for the day,
resist my demons within and let the rest of the world prey.

In the crucible of my mind, I wage a relentless strife,
Adorning a facade as I venture into life.
Against inner demons, I fiercely contend,
While the world outside seeks to bend.

With fortitude and determination, I face each day,
Combatting shadows, that obscure my way.
Though doubts assail and fears persist,
I stand resolute, refusing to desist.

Behind a veil, I cloak my inner turmoil,
Navigating life's labyrinth with unyielding toil.
For within me, a tempest rages on,
Yet outwardly, I display a façade, calm and strong.

Let the world scheme, let it scrutinize and pry,
I shall confront the chaos, I shall defy.

2. Journey on

Beneath the waves, where pressure binds,
I struggle, gasping, in depths unkind.
Surrounded by silence, a world apart,
In the ocean's embrace, with a heavy heart.

In the void of space, where emptiness reigns,
I drift aimlessly, amid cosmic plains.
No air to breathe, no ground below,
Just endless darkness, where shadows float.

Upon the clouds, where dreams take flight,
I soar, weightless, in the sky's soft light.
But storms may gather, and winds may blow,
Testing my resolve, in highs and lows.

Atop the mountains, where peaks scrape the sky,
I climb, relentless, though the summit's nigh.
Each step a struggle, each breath a prayer,
In the rugged terrain, where challenges glare.

Through depths and heights, I journey on,
Facing trials, until the break of dawn.

AAROHI BHATTACHARYA

For in each suffering, a lesson learned,
And strength renewed, as the tides are turned.

3. Walls of trust

In the realm of trust, I built a wall,
Each brick laid with care, it stood so tall.
Time was spent, it's strength grew strong,
Yet, in an instant, it all went wrong.

Like glass it shattered, fragile and fast,
Leaving me, to ponder the past.
What if instead, a home of glass I'd made,
To shield from falseness, a refuge laid?

Transparent walls, revealing truth's light,
Protecting from the shadows of deceit's might.
To capture oneself in such clarity,
Isolation from the false, a sanctuary.

So let's rebuild, not with bricks of doubt,
But with transparency, inside and out.
For in a glass home, we find the key,
To trust, to honesty, to truly be free.

4. Yearning to feel life

In twilight's hush, Death longed for life,
To feel the sun, escape his strife.
He reached to touch a rose's bloom,
But with his touch, brought silent doom.

The petals wilted, colors bled,
The flower drooped, its fragrance fled.
Death's heart ached with a mournful cry,
For beauty lost with just one try.

"Oh, to breathe the morning's dew,
To feel the world in vibrant hue,
But all I touch must fade and fall,
I bring the end, the final call."

Regret and guilt filled his core,
For life's warm touch he'd know no more.
Death turned away with heavy sigh,
Longing to live, but bound to die.

5. The unfinished tale

Amid walls of mirrors, in solace I dwell,
Where echoes of silence weave a spell.
Lying on the floor, papers unfold,
An unfinished tale, it's secrets untold.
Forgotten and torn, these pages weep,
Yet within their creases, dreams leap.
Each word a thought, beneath the moon's glow,
A new story emerges, from dust below.
To finish the tale, my only desire,
Yet the past holds flames, fueled by fire.
Fear grips tight, the uncertain end,
As I tread softly, around the bend.
On floors of fate, where papers reside,
In the dance of dubiety, I'll confide,
I journey onward, with nothing to hide,
For in embracing the unknown, true courage is allied.

6. Riverside Reflections

The blue of your eyes reminds me of the river I sat by recently,
Which flowed and filled me with scarce serenity,
It wasn't the noise but the voice of your heart that matched the
rhythm of the water.
Oh how unclear was it, my reflection, yet when it stopped at the
corner
I could see the clear signs of change.
In that mirror of truth I learned mindfulness,
Was taught how satisfaction is the ultimate longing of life,
How no other happiness of goods could fill in that space within.
The texture of your skin reminds me of the trees I saw
Of the flowers that bloomed and also of the leaves withering and
falling
And oh how you smiled, reminded me of the freedom one yearns
while breathing.
Captured in this body is a soul, waiting to be everything at once,
Yet aware of the illusion it stays silent, waiting to be anything at
all.

7. Façade of Perception

In life's grand gallery, faces paint the walls,
Eyes like hawks, we judge as it falls.
A glance, a siren's call, whispering allure,
First impressions bind us, though hearts are pure.

Masked in silken shades, truth hides in disguise,
We vow to see within, but sight betrays our eyes.
A rose amidst the thorns we see, beauty's hidden thread it is so
meek,
The cover judged, the story left unread.
Mirrors of the mind, shallow streams they play,
Ripples of perception, distortions in our way.
Beneath the surface sheen, the essence we forsake,
The ghost of first impressions, our human hearts at stake.

Yet as dusk descends, a truth begins to rise,
Beauty's but a portal, a riddle in our eyes.
For in the beholder's gaze, the spirit wends its way,
Beyond the fleeting forms, where true connections lay.
So take your time, it could all be a lie.
It could've been or yourself in your sight.

8. Beware traveler

Beware, dear traveler, for death awaits,
A peaceful state called Heaven's gate.
The journey of life, a windning road,
With no destination, no final abode.
Through valleys dark and mountains high,
We journey on beneath the sky.
Each step we take, a fleeting breath,
In the dance of life, between birth and death.
Beware, dear traveler, of fleeting time,
For every moment, a precious chime.
The sand of fate slips through our hands,
As we wander through unkown lands.
Walking in the woods where music fills the air,
In that melody of life, we weave our share.
But Death, dear traveler, is always near,
A reminder that our end is clear.
So cherish each sunrise, each twlight's gleam,
For life is but a fleeting dream.
Beware, dear traveler, as you roam,
For a new beginning awaits us all, to lead us home.

9. Is everything gonna be alright ?

When you think that it's gonna be all right
but then you're punched hard and you can't stand,
Then you know it was just the silence before the storm and it
ain't gonna end
It starts with the dark night
Hundreds and thousands of falling kites
When you know that a second would seem like years
Because obviously it's a lie that time passes by.
When you are too busy to care
Then emerges a bunch of dares
To let you feel the immense pain deep down there.
When you know you aren't a rock
And you can't just cope up with the shock
It's blocked you know the one and only way it's locked.
When you're blind to the colors of the world
The world other than the fantasy one
And the reality is only black and white
From which you can't even run.
And when you think it's finally alright
There is this kick that flies

And this feels worse,
Worse than a wicked witch's curse
When the witch has no antidote
And you're rotten to the core
That's when your blood just feels icy cold.
Why am I in a place where I certainly don't belong
There is this deep thirst and quenching it is what I long.
I know it's God's mistake
He sent me to the wrong place
That is when you ultimately think that this is a better place
You know that there's hardly any bigger disgrace.
Can I ask you God if I am alive
Because I don't feel like it and I just can't act like it,
Until and unless I find someone to hold me
To pull me from the cold me
To make me the bold me
To save me from sinking
And just stop me overthinking.
Until and unless I am done with my insecurities
E'll be right by my side showing me the possibilities .
Yes I am a murderer
If a murderer is someone who kills the dead
Who makes the already silent go to bed
Who tosses the knife again and again
Thinking if the torture is ever gonna end.
Tell me is it me or you who killed her
The naive and innocent pretty little girl.

Fine it was me who bought her devil out I agree
But it was important as she wanted to be free.
I was lost and wandering
It was all in my head
Like a nightmare, a bad dream that
I can never forget.
I want somebody, to be the one and only
To tell me "If ever you're afraid you will... always find me"
Holding my hand and whispering in my ear
"Its gonna be alright there's nothing to fear."
"It's gonna be alright there's nothing to fear."

10. Even in laughter the heart may ache

Shattered into fragments,
like shards of glass cascading down,
I descend into the depths,
laughter bubbling from lips tinged with sorrow.
Calling out to the one weeping within,
a reflection of demons unseen.
Tears mingle with rain,
wet soaking cheeks, heavy with the weight of unspoken fears.
Each night, a dance with the unknown,
fear lurking creeping tendrils of dread,
caressing the edges of consciousness.
In the cemetery of my mind,
creatures of the night slither and crawl,
their whispers echoing through the darkness,
as I chuckle, a hollow sound of what's lost.
Clouds pulse with a heartbeat
syncopated with the missing rhythm of my own.
flickering memories etched in age-worn hues
hover in the liminal spaces of my mind.

A whirlwind of emotions slices through,
tearing at the fabric of my being,
he, a ghost of the past,
haunting my thoughts with pretty lies.
There I see a Canary take flight,
it's wings a symphony of freedom,
a distant dream in a world of disillusionment,
where truth is but a fleeting shadow.
Crying, screaming, laughing,
the cacophony of hysteria surrounds,
yet amidst the chaos, a whisper of hope leads to life,
a glimmer of light in the darkness of the soul.

11. Symphony of futility

Come stay in my head for a day,
and witness the demons' relentless howls,
their cries a ceaseless dirge to my futility.
I've learned that to feel so deeply is a curse,
a malevolent force with colossal claws,
rending happiness into shreds.

This curse, birthed from within
haunting my existence,
killing me anew each day.
Or perhaps, madness gripped me once more,
as delusional fears echo like Macbeth's phantom.

We are living dead, trapped yet unburied,
their soul yearning for life while ours extinguish.
Entombed in soil, we scream for freedom,
but unlike them, who rest alone,
we suffer in our shared loneliness.

12. Summon

In shadows deep and darkness around,
I know there's light for it to be found.
Earth whispers softly, a solemn ring.
Grave's silent stir, voices keen,
A haunting melody, in the quiet of soil.
The buried summon, the living chase,
I wandered with corpses yet in the haze.
Where's the path, I know not,
In this mist I've been caught.
Yes, you've been summoned
Yes, they'd been called...

13. Kalyug

We know not time,
We know not love,
We're all scattering
Like this expanding universe.

All shall fall apart,
Nothing shall remain,
The remnants must decay,
The trusted would betray.

The destroyer would
Let there be poignancy,
Kalki shall seek revenge
In a dance of destiny.

Humans may not understand
Life in its final stand
That'll be when the ultimate silence overpowers

As the darkness takes it's hour.

14. Lost in the echoes of longing

When sickness grips and tiredness reigns,
Love's warmth like sunshine, soothes the pains.
Yearning for someone to light up your world,
To turn the darkest nights into unfurled.

But he, indifferent, offers no solace,
His apathy cuts deeper than malice.
Words, like knives, stab at your core,
His icy gaze, a tempest's roar.

Toxicity lingers in every glance,
Leaving scars too deep for mere chance.
Dreams of openness, of shared delight,
Shattered by his callous slight.

Yet not all desires find their way,
Sometimes they're shadows, fading gray.
In the fairy lights, dreams dance and sway,
But some hearts remain cold, come what may.

Not every whisper can banish the night,
Not every touch can make things right.
For in the depths where darkness lies,
Not all can see through tear-filled eyes.

15. Just A Story

THE HEART WAS NEVER MINE TO TAKE

All those years I studied how to steal a heart, gently, skillfully,

without leaving too much behind.

Once I saw her, I knew I was ready.

I brought her flowers. I whispered promises.

Each time I did,

I saw how her eyes, still as they were,

reflected the light falling on the glass above her, as if she knew I

was coming.

And when they gave me the key,

I opened her cage with hands that trembled like prayer.

She didn't speak. Not a word.

But silence can be consent

when you need it to be, can it not?

I had practiced for this.

Quick, clean, precise,

I would not fumble.

But when I reached for her heart,

it wasn't there.

Gone.

Removed without a trace.

He had already been here.

And he must've been so cruel,
NO scar,
NO bandage,
NO blood.
Just Pain…
But not me.
I stayed.
I washed her,
dirt still fresh on my boots,
blood beneath my nails.
I wrapped her carefully,
put her back in her glass bed.
And I told myself I was better,
because I cared…
After the damage was done.
I brought a bouquet this time.
Not in hope, but in apology.
For never asking
if she even had a heart left to give.
Then I gave up.
I cleaned my blade.
Used the same shovel
to open the earth again.
And I lay down, on top of her,
pressing into what was left,
seeking warmth in a body
that could no longer feel.

Oh, how hard must I have fallen.
For here I am, breathing, free, and buried.
I searched for something in her face,
some sign she knew. There was nothing.
None to begin with, I doubt.
So I lay there,
still as the soil closing over us,
accepting that even the right one
can come at the wrong time.
And I smiled,
and frowned,
wondering what he's doing now-
with the heart
that could've been mine,
THE HEART THAT SHOULD'VE BEEN MINE….

16. Carve your story

In the silent caves where life meets its end,
You seek the essence that death may lend.
But find only thoughts in the depths
Where echoes of breath once danced fair.

Reader, grasp the fleeting moment's flame,
Forge your path in the face of time's game.
Each step a testament to your legacy's bloom,
In the tapestry of eternity's infinite room.

With passion's fire and courage's might,
Carve your story in the dark of night.
For life's brief candle flickers and wanes,
But the soul's song forever remains.

So heed the call of destiny's plea,
Before it's late and you regret to be.
In the grand symphony of cosmic design,
Be the melody that transcends time.

17. Hades' Realm

In the realm of Hades, veins weave
A web where you speak of it, you challenge belief,
You think of it, you're inviting it
For in the knowledge of darkness it is that you value that light.

Time, energy, mind, longevity's dance,
In Hades' realm, where shadows advance,
Everything that kills, makes you feel alive,
In the depths of despair, where souls strive.

They say, talking of the dark, it pulls you near,
Gradually, it whispers, drawing you clear,
Why is it wrong to seek the light's gleam,
After knowing darkness, in its silent scream?

Human tendency, an echo of stars,
An extension of the cosmos, bound by bars,
Delve deeper, dive down, to the core,
Where ancient whispers, echo once more.

Our past, their future, intertwined,
Before the end, seek what's defined,

In Hades' realm, where shadows thrive,
Seek the light, where souls revive.

18. Waves of grief

Grief, a tempest upon life's sea,
In waves it comes, relentless decree.
When the ship of joy is wrecked, undone,
You're left adrift, beneath the sun.

At first, the waves, towering high,
Crash upon you, no respite nigh.
Every person, each deed
Comes to life as beauty recedes.

You cling to wreckage, memories dear,
A lifeline in the chaos, ever near.
Hold on, just float, amidst the storm,
In the tumultuous sea, grief takes form.

The waves, they rage, a hundred feet tall,
Crushing, relentless, upon all.
But in the depths, a flicker of hope lies,
Between the waves, a chance to cope lies.

Weeks pass, maybe months, the waves still fierce,
Yet farther apart, granting a pierce.

In the calm, you find your breath as you float,
Amidst the chaos of that moment's depth.

Triggers abound, unexpected and swift,
A song, a scent, a memory's gift.
The wave crashes in, relentless and stark,
But in its wake, you find the spark.

Life persists, amidst the strife,
In between waves, the pulse of life.
Grief, a journey, with twists and bends,
But in the pauses, life transcends.

19. Destiny's Dance

On the surface, where mysteries roam,
We dance as puppets, in the unknown's home.
Strings unseen, pulled by fate's gentle hand,
Guiding our steps across life's shifting strands.

We think we're masters, of our own design,
Yet destiny's whispers weave a grander line.
Each choice we make, each path we tread,
Echoes a script already read.

From birth to death, we play our part,
Bound by the strings of a cosmic art.
Yet in our hearts, a flicker of light,
A spark of hope, in the darkest night,
That yes we choose, we've got a choice
That it'll end up different and I'll have a voice.

For though we're puppets, in the grand scheme,
We hold the power to dream and redeem.
To carve our path through the unknown's mist,
And find our purpose, in the dance we enlist.

20. Scars

Scars etched deep, where time can't heal,
A silent ache, that hearts conceal.
Time, a currency borrowed, we spend,
Yet wounds linger, without an end.

How obvious the lie, that time flies,
As pain persists, beneath the skies.
Memories haunt, like ghosts unseen,
In the vast expanse, where dreams convene.

Each scar a story, etched in skin,
A testament to where we've been.
Time's illusion, a fleeting sigh,
For scars remain, though days pass by.

So let us embrace, our wounds and flaws,
For they're reminders, of life's raw applause.
So don't pass it on and still be kind for these are
The scars that shape us, in heart and mind.

21. Flames of fire

I've got that fire in me
Of which am scared,
Scared that it'll burn you,
Burn us down to ashes.
Yet you hold onto me,
Reminding me that I light up your world,
That the fire in me kills the dark in you,
But that devil in me is quietly waiting,
To prove you wrong and throw you in
The tartarus in the fire of this hell
You're the ice that keeps me cold
That lets me stand on my own
You are all I need to burn
Our hearts are burnt, yours of ice, mine due to fire
Yet our souls unite in a realm thats higher
In my heart a flame flickers bright
A fire that burns with passion and light
It's a power that's wild and true
A vigour that's fierce and pure and new

22. The last beautiful thing

In shadows deep, where nothing lies,
The last beautiful thing caught my eye.
A fleeting glimpse, a radiant glow,
Yet its brilliance brought me woe.

'Twas not the sun, nor stars above,
But a beauty unmatched, a sight to love.
Yet in its grace, a cruel decree,
For its splendor was too much for me.

Blinded by its dazzling hue,
I stumbled forth, my vision askew.
For in that moment, beauty's sting
Left me with naught but memories to cling.

Fair beauty, thy visage doth beguile,
Yet within thy grasp, lies treacherous guile.
For in thy splendor, a deceitful smile,
That leads me down, a perilous aisle.
That was the last beautiful thing I saw,

Which blurred my vision for sure.

23. Seasons of the soul

In springtime's bloom, with skies so fair,
We greet the world, without a care.
Like buds unfurling, hearts take flight,
In love's sweet embrace, our souls unite.

But summer's heat soon takes its toll,
The fire of passion, burns the soul.
Yet amidst the blaze, we find our way,
And bask in the warmth of love's bright ray.

Then autumn comes, with colors bold,
The winds of change, they take their hold.
We face the harvest, with bittersweet sighs,
As memories fade, and old dreams die.

And in the winter of our years,
We face the truth, and shed our tears.
Yet in the cold, there lies a grace,
A wisdom earned, in life's new face.

So let us journey, come what may,
Through seasons of life, in night and day.

AAROHI BHATTACHARYA

For in the end, what will remain,
Are echoes of love, and memories gained.

24. "If my life is going to mean anything, I have to live it myself."

Limitations I never crossed
It brought tears in my eyes
and made me think (about me) twice
(It happened)for the first time in my life
(And I wondered) If all of them were just lies.
I hope not, I can't take more.
Its already hard to make four out of the two.
Its hard to try and not believe
But its harder to deny the truth when you know
It is what it is.
Nothing more nothing less.
I won't take another step
I thought I could but now it ended
Way better than what I'd expected
No fights, no riots and no denials
Just a hug, goodbye and farewells
When will this stop making me pretend.
I dont know what I want and what I can get

AAROHI BHATTACHARYA

I never thought this time it wasn't all set
The worst memories are to see the people you've made memories
with become memories....
Doesn't it feel good to be alone
Dark at heart and black at soul.

25. Blind sighted

I ain't blind to the tears
I ain't deaf to the noise
I can feel freaking torture
I can hear my own voice..

I am lying to myself
When I say I am done
Cause I know my heart
Will start to beat in a second.

How could someone be
Such a nightmare to me
Yet such an angel as if ran right out of my dreams
If only it were true to be, for at all times have I seen
Is the kind of demon you've been...

26. "A thing of beauty is a joy forever."

I'd love to keep your soul forever
If forever means it lasts
If that's the final destiny
If that's the power we cast
The thing of beauty it'll be,
A joy forever till we're free.
I hope I get the heart I desire
Such it doesn't burn us down in thy blazing fire
Such that we don't lose ourselves
Amidst the raising hatred, crept
Creatures right from the hell
Right when we've aleady lept.
So let's get back to where we belong
With the moon and sun singing our song.

27. Drowning Deep

In the depths of life's relentless sea, I drown,
Weighted by gloom, regret, and sorrow's crown.
Lost in swirling currents, where shadows creep,
Silent waves of dreams that I can't keep.
Water fills my lungs, suffocating soul,
Regret's undertow pulls me from my goal.
Darkness surrounds, a cold and crushing hold,
Alone in this abyss, where hope grows cold.
Drowning not in water, but in deep despair,
Echoes of mistakes fill the murky air.
Will I break the surface, find light's sweet sound,
Or sink deeper, where darkness knows no bound?

28. Conceal

Oh, how delightful it is to hide emotions away,
In the depths of our hearts, where they silently decay.
With smiles plastered on, and laughter in tow,
We parade through life, hiding what we know.

How amusing it is to play this game,
Where we bury our feelings, but they're never the same.
We joke and we jest, with a cynical air,
While inside we're crumbling, beyond repair.

So let's raise a toast to this façade we maintain,
Where we laugh on the outside, but inside, we're in pain.
Oh, what a riot it is, to hide what's within,
As we sink in our sorrow, with a sarcastic grin.

29. Autumn

In the aftermath of rain, autumn sighs,
Leaves glisten, kissed by droplets from the sky.
As nature's palette shifts to hues of amber, gold, and shades of
crimson,
Falling softly from the swaying trees,
They scatter, they dance, they rustle and closely listen.
The scent of earth rises, oh and the breeze,
Misty veils adorn the distant hills,
As twilight casts its spell, the world grows still.
In this tranquil moment, beauty reigns supreme,
A symphony of sights and sounds, a dream.
So let us wander through this painted scene,
Where every step reveals a new serene.

30. Lies

You stop fearing hell
When you've been through it
When you've loved someone
Who belongs to it.
Each one of us is a devil in disguise
No matter how much he tries
He'll be tied to his lies
Never pleased nor satisfied.
Its the pain they have to bear
Their fake clothing all the layers
Will be withered and all teared
Then you'll know life's playing well
Its a game to keep you in the hell.

31. Haze in the maze

I won't say life isn't just,
But here, cruelty is a must.
Today I felt my soul's deep howl,
A scream, a sob, a silent growl.

No tears to fall, but body quakes,
In silent storms that heartbreak makes.
It's hard to listen, hold my peace,
When silence fuels the fires increase.

Words unspoken, thoughts confined,
I still believe my existence isn't blind.
Fear of failure haunts my days,
I don't want death, but life's malaise.

Surrounded yet profoundly lone,
No shoulder here to call my own.
Lonely, not alone I feel,
Yearning for a bond that's real.

Everyone seeks heaven's door,
But none would die to settle the score.

Villains born from endless pain,
I see now how they're forged in flame.

To have a soul see deep within,
Without a word, the bond begin.
Questions asked, but none that see,
Their asking only burdens me.

Deaf like Hades, blind as night,
Numb in sorrow's endless flight.
Hurt and useless, guilt consumes,
Falling like a corpse in tombs.

Rotten is this hell on earth,
Misery weighs down my worth.
For me, the rain's a sweet escape,
Too cold, forget, let sorrow drape.

32. Why me ?

In the hollow, I find my mind entwined,
A heart in torment, seeking peace to find.
I hate myself for being who I am,
And dislike my mom for birthing me.

I hate my friends for all the care they show,
Their kindness feels like mockery's cruel blow.
I hate the world for saying I'm no worth,
These words they hurl have anchored me to earth.

I hate him for his words that cut so deep,
"You don't deserve to be," haunts in my sleep.
And her complaints, a knife that twists inside,
In every wound, I hear the voices chide.

Shouldn't they think before their words take flight?
Their careless tongues inflict a lasting blight.
Don't they know how it feels to question life,
To wish for end, to cease the endless strife?

Each day I wear a mask, a hollow grin,
Pretend I'm happy, while it rots within.

Confusion reigns, I struggle to find why,
Why I'm here at all, beneath this empty sky.

"Why me, Mom?" I ask, "Why did you bear?"
A silent plea to end this deep despair.

33. Inside and out

Why is it so dark inside and out
This dark night has no ray of hope
What is it all about
Who is it that I can't stay without.
Am I the culprit did I ruin everything
This is what I now highly doubt.
Why is it so quiet inside and out
Or am I just missing the loud shouts from the crowd
That once in the same life made me feel so proud.
I never vowed that I will ask for permissions or ask if I am
allowed,
But there are so many problems that I can't even count.
I just know that my every prayer will be heard,
Every tear will be seen and every heartache felt,
That yes maybe someday it's love by which am held.

34. Shatter me

Folded within the pages, I reside,
In books, my solace, where worlds collide.
Bonds with paper characters, deep and strong,
In stories, I find where I belong.

Love and loss intertwined in history's tale,
The moon, steadfast, in the night's veil.
A constant companion, watching our strife,
Changing as we do, in the dance of life.

The world, a flat expanse, I've fallen through,
Grasping for hands, in the dark's ensue.
Numbness seeps in, as raindrops patter,
As the chilling cold and wind shatters.

In darkness, we reveal our truest form,
Butterflies flutter, in the midst of the storm.
Hope bleeds from wounds, inflicted by truth,
In the silent night, we seek our youth.

Cursed and gifted, in equal measure,
A touch that's lethal, a hidden treasure.

A weapon forged, in the fires of night,
Seeking redemption, in dawn's first light.

• 52 •

35. Fear not

Fear kills before failure does,
Fire's still and the ice above,
Strength within had never been us,
It is what we fight for success and love.

36. I don't want to be accepted if you can't accept me the way I am !

I don't want acceptance that demands I change,
I have one life, and its course is mine to arrange.
No belief in rebirth, no second try,
I'll live my truth, not society's lie.

I hear the comments, the critiques, the praise,
But no one's perfect in their myriad ways.
So how can they judge, who themselves are flawed?
I won't mold myself for their applause.

If acceptance means changing who I am,
Then I'd rather stay true, with a heart unscanned.
I'll walk with the Lord, let Him guide,
Not the voices that seek to decide.

One life I have, and it's mine to live,
So I ask of you, this freedom give.
Live your own life, and let me be,

For I don't seek acceptance if you can't accept me.

Dawn's Resurgence

37. Shine

Its so unclear
Yet today that's all I wish to see.
That cold is so chilly
Yet sometimes that's what I want to feel.
The wind is so wild,
Yet in its chaos, I find a strange comfort.
The rain is so heavy
Yet at times that's all I need to bury myself into.
The night is so dark
Yet at times that's where I find myself.
It feels so lonely
I feel so distant
Yet when I look at the stars
I realize each one has a separate place to shine.
And every shadow has a purpose to cast.

38. From Ashes to Us

I fell like ashes to the ground

Then it was me whom you found

With my head in my hands and dejected looking eyes

You felt like helping after you perceived my inaudible cries.

You knew you meant nothing to me at that time

But still you bowed down to assist this frail vanquished vine.

Woefully you stumbled and fumbled to see my roots

Only to find that they're strong and won't let me move.

Still you bruised yourself to set me free

from my never ending thoughts and dispirited me.

At first you didn't seem very gratifying or nice

But I could read the clear signs of acceptance in your eyes.

I believed I pulled you down to this hell

Since I could see you drown, dwell and rebel.

You were crushed to death and faced the Tartarus,

Still you struggled to lift me and created the 'us'.

I wonder how we never brawled,

Seems like we were close, together when we crawled.

We ignored each other's atrocious trait

To see where it lead us, our fate.

I feel certain that even if we don't talk for an aeon,

We will be together at heart n soul

And I'll be there for you from dusk till dawn.

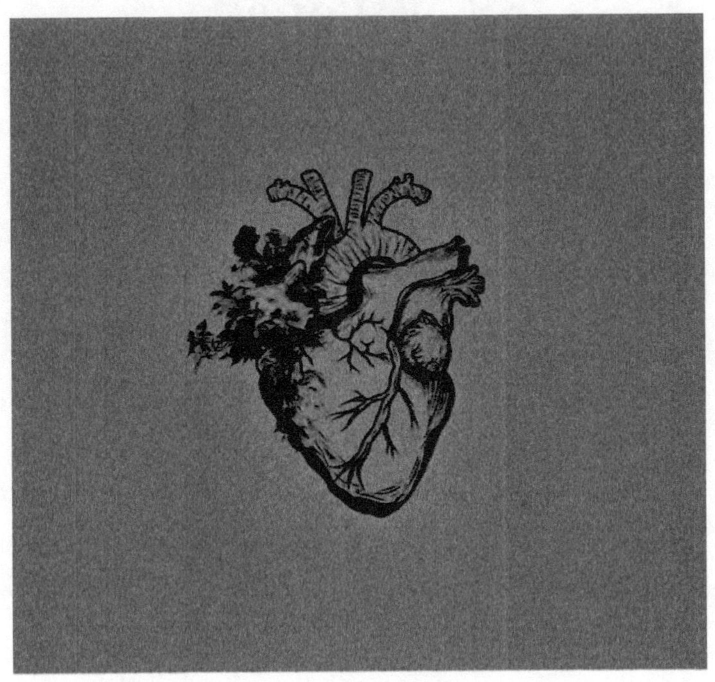

39. Villanelle

I will not have you without your shadows,
Those murky depths that linger in your piercing gaze,
For they are the echoes of your past,
The whispers of your fears,
And within them lies the essence of your being.

I will not let you have me without my chaos,
The swirling storm that rages within,
For it is the furnace of my passion,
The catalyst of my creativity,
And within it resides the core of my soul.

If our demons cannot dance,
Then neither can our angels soar,
For they are two sides of the same coin,
And in their intertwined embrace,
We find the balance of our being.

For in their delicate interplay,
We discover the essence of who we are.
She'll forever be girl in love with the dark hearts,
old souls and the melancholy of Edgar Allan Poe.

40. Near yet far away

In those deep black eyes, familiarity lies,
A silent echo of shared skies.
The face, unreadable, yet strangely near,
Whispers of memories, crystal clear.

Lips once cherished, a touch so longed,
In their warmth, a melody belonged.
A voice, a tether to the soul's embrace,
Binding hearts in an unspoken grace.

Words woven like threads, enchanting the soul,
Drawing closer, making us whole.
In the dance of connection, we find our fall,
In the echoes of familiarity, we heed the call.

You're so near yet so far away
That I feel the pain and still laugh my way.

41. Dawn's embrace

On a gentle morn, as misty dreams unfurl,
And Irish whispers dance with the swirl,
Thunder rumbles, a voice within roars,
Echoing truth, unlocking closed doors.
Raindrops cascade, a gentle embrace,
Washing away each tear-stained trace,
She stands in the downpour, feeling anew,
Bathed in the solace of skies so true.
Each drop a memory, each storm a tale,
Of trials endured, of strength unveiled,
For in the rain, she finds her release,
A symphony of sorrows, a sweet peace.
Her tears, like rivers, flow and drain,
Yet from the depths, she'll rise again,
For within the storm, she finds her voice,
A melody of courage, a fearless choice.
And when the rainbow arcs the sky,
A promise whispered, a lullaby,
"Awake, dear soul, embrace the light,
Turn darkness into dawn, take your flight."

42. Surviving with Purpose

In every tempest life has hurled my way,
I've met it laughing, braving fierce the gale,
Surviving, yet yearning for a brighter day,
Seeking deeper purpose, beyond the pale.
Each storm, a test, a trial to endure,
Yet laughter echoes through the darkest night,
Within eyes of mine, a tale of bravery so pure,
A witness to the battles, won with might.
Oh, may my life find meaning in the strife,
Beyond mere survival, a greater call,
To rise above, to soar beyond this life,
To leave a legacy, to stand tall.
So let the storms rage on, I'll face them bold,
With laughter as my shield, my heart unrolled.

43. Love's eternal lamp

If only I knew what you meant,
When you said you could listen to me for ages,
Would love to see me grow old,
And stay blind to my beauty outside.

Your words, a tender whisper,
Promised love beyond time,
A bond unbroken by years,
A connection deeper than sight.

To stay blind yet truly see,
The essence of who I am,
A beauty unseen, but felt,
In love's eternal lamp.

44. Celestial call

Sunlight spills through morn's gentle veil,
The river winds with silver in its wake.
Windy mountains stand with ancient might,
While twisted trees and bushes whisper low.
The crescent moon drapes twilight in soft grace,
Moonlight dances on the tranquil land.
Shimmering stars adorn the midnight sky,
All call to me in silent, timeless song.
In their embrace, I hear the earth's own voice,
A symphony of nature's endless call.

45. Envying

In jealousy's murky depths, I'm submerged,
A nightmare's grip tightens, a ghostly whisper lingers,
Underwater, I drown, I struggle against envy's tide,
Gasping for air, but finding only darkness.
The weight of comparison pulls me deeper,
Each wave a reminder of what I lack,
A ghost of my insecurities drifts by,
Haunting every thought, every moment.
In this watery abyss, I am alone,
Bound by jealousy's relentless hold,
No surface in sight, no escape from the depths,
Just the cold embrace of envy's sea.

46. The mirage of reality

Life's journey, a winding path,
Between perception's veil and reality's wrath.
Illusions dance, truths unfold,
In the story of life, both young and old.

Perception's prism, colors bright,
Reality's mirror, reflecting light.
In the dance of shadows, we find our way,
Navigating the realms, night and day.

An endless journey, with twists and turns,
Where perception shifts, and reality burns.
In the balance between what we see and feel,
Lies the essence of life, raw and real.

47. Memory lane

In the quiet depths of solitude, I dwell,
Where silence reigns, and whispers swell.
I choose to love you here, where no rejection stings,
For in the canvas of dreams, you're mine alone.

In the sanctuary of whispered pleas,
I hold you close, where no one sees.
Memories intertwine in the prison of thought,
A past promised, yet fate's design.

You danced into my world, a fleeting wisp,
A vision of love, a bittersweet kiss.
Yet your voice remains unheard,
By the icy grip of silence, deferred.

You drifted beyond the horizon's reach,
Leaving an ache, a silent breach.
Beneath the starlit sky, I stand alone,
In the memory lane of love, forever known.

So I choose to love you in silence's embrace,
Where heartache leaves not a trace.

AAROHI BHATTACHARYA

In dreams, you're mine, and mine alone,
In the sanctuary of the night we have sown.

48. Eternal snapshots

In photographs, time's fleeting moments lie,
Captured still, they whisper tales of the past.
They journey through the years, beneath the sky,
Where memories and echoes are amassed.
So live with no excuses, free and vast,
Embrace each day as if it were the last.
For in the end, regret's a shadowed debt
Travel far, and in your heart, don't forget.

49. Journey through time

In frames of memories, photographs reside,
Capturing moments, where hearts coincide.
They travel through time, in a silent ballet,
Reminding us of moments that won't sway.
So live without excuses, embrace the now,
For time's relentless march, we can't disavow.
Travel without regret, let wanderlust ignite,
Explore the world's wonders, day or night.
So seize the day with passion's flame,
Embrace the journey, without blame.
Let photographs be windows to the past,
As we travel through time, our memories vast.

50. The paradox: Love and Hate

In the shadows of disdain, love's twisted twin,
A paradox of passion, where hate begins.
Each thought, a knot, tightly bound,
In the heart's silent battleground.

With every glance, a stab of pain,
Yet echoes of affection still remain.
The line between love and hate blurs,
In the stormy sea where emotions stir.

For to hate is to care, in a twisted way,
To feel the pull, yet push away.
A dance of contradictions, tangled and torn,
In the labyrinth of emotions, we're born.

So in the depths of loathing, there lies,
A hidden truth beneath disguise.
For hating someone, strangely enough,
Resembles the intensity of love's rough.

51. Canvas of life

Life is a canvas, vast and unblemished,
Where moments paint the shifting tide.
Each day adds a hue, each choice a stroke,
Weaving together an artistic quest.

In time's palette, colors blend and shift,
Shades of joy and sorrow interlace.
With every laugh and tear,
We leave our mark, visible and clear.

Bright strokes of laughter stand out,
Vivid and bold, capturing our joy.
Yet shadows drift in subtle grays,
Moments of darkness along the journey.

The canvas of life is resilient,
Each layer of paint tells a story.
In the interplay of light and dark,
We discover beauty, the essence of our journey.

So let us paint with passion and grace,
Not concealing our true face.

For in the end, when our canvas is done,
Our life's masterpiece will be brightly shun.

52. Memories

They say the worst part of holding a memory is not the pain it carries but the loneliness of it. Sharing a memory is as joyful as making one. Yet, the worst memory is watching the people you have made memories with become memories themselves.

53. Welcome to society

Welcome to society's grand stage,
Where rules and norms oft engage,
We bid you enter, hope you'll thrive,
Yet beware the paths where we connive.

Feel free to be yourself, we say,
But tread with care, choose your own way,
Love your body, but not too bold,
For arrogance, we'll swiftly scold.

We'll mock your joy, question your smile,
Then lament when sadness you compile,
Whispers of worthlessness, so profound,
Yet we'll cry when you're in the ground.

Love, oh love, it's a wondrous thing,
But let us choose who wears the ring,
Opinions, yes, you're free to share,
But align them with our collective stare.

Welcome to society's embrace,
Where promises hide a twisted face,

AAROHI BHATTACHARYA

Once you're in, there's no reprieve,
For leaving? Oh no, you cannot leave.

54. Truth too lies

Live the beautiful lie with wise,
For once the truth settles the ugly death lies.
In life's mosaic, beauty weaves through,
guiding us with bright smiles.
We dance in blissful ignorance,
unaware of shadows beneath.
Death waits, ready to shatter illusions,
while we cling to transient charm.
Savor each breath, heed the quiet call
truth endures beyond life's sweet lie.

55. Milestones

In the journey of life, I seek milestones,
They ignite a spark of hope within,
Assuring me, I'll soon reach my destination,
Each one a testament to progress made.

Just as the joy of completing small goals,
Brings a smile to my face,
They whisper softly, "One step closer,
To the sweet taste of success."

With each milestone conquered,
I find strength to carry on,
For in their presence lies the promise,
Of dreams fulfilled and battles won.

56. To the loved one

Oh, my loved one,
I want you to come to me as naturally as I breathe.
I want to be felt like the ushered wind against my skin.
I want to be seen, stripped, as I am when I stand drenched in
rain—
not of clothes, but of masks.
I want no façade, no faces,
no feelings that were never mine.
Oh, loved one,
I want you to live for yourself, and through that, live for me.
I want you to laugh with me,
laugh as if sadness were never known,
laugh for me like you have never been happier.
I want you to be the scent I find even in the most impossible
places—
a scent so strong my heart hurts when it is gone.
Oh, dearest loved one,
whether you are a soul, a mountain, a fleeting feeling,
or the voice of the universe itself—oh God—
if ever you must leave,
I pray you shed no tears.
(And somewhere between those words, I pray for myself too.)

For the right one does not always meet the right time.
I promise I will not hold you too tightly.
If you are meant to stay, you will.
And if you must leave,
I will not stop you.
I will let you go.
And in that surrender,
I will find the kindest kind of love.
Oh, pray, oh loved one,
I promise to let you feel freely, never to bind you to me.
So that when you do feel, it will be true,
and never something forced.
I promise to try—
try to be there always,
try to take you far away from loneliness,
try to heal you and heal myself in the process,
try to break you free from your darkest thoughts.
Every time, every night, in every way I can,
I promise I will be willing to keep you.
Oh yes, my loved one,
whether you are another soul,
the mountains I ache for,
the peace of a forest,
the whisper of the universe,
or the part of myself still learning to love—
one day, I will smile, and call it love.
Not blind, but seeing.

Not binding, but freeing.
I will be kind to many,
but vulnerable to one.
I will act my age with the world,
but be my true self with one.
I will speak and hear the many voices calling,
but I will pour my heart out, and truly listen to just one—
You, my loved one.
It was, is, and will be you, my loved one.

57. Yearnings of a soul in the rain

*Drenching in the rain hiding the tears and my wet soaked cheeks
in the moonlight during the nightfall under the burning stars in
the open sky in the shade of the dark clouds, I long for it.*

*I long for a new tale in the scorching sunlight under the trees
with my shadow alone to end.
Among the laughing kids cheering up the upset is what I long for*

.

*I crave to stay in the village talking to the elderly speaking less of
myself and yet hearing all the stories they wish to share.
Yes to write them down in the lampshade is what I long for.*

*To paint a tapestry so vivid, brilliant and colorful on a black
and white canvas, to capture the moments I wish to live again
through cameras is what I crave.*

*I yearn to smile at my swaying hair and falling leaves in the
wind of the autumn, to speak to myself, explain what I want
and what am tired of that is something I will do.*

I live not to survive, live to cherish these small yet significant memories. Loving self, yet living with others to attain happiness, to be a part of this society and to act as a change is what I look for in myself...

Reflect

-Catherine Fisher

"A seed hidden in the heart of an apple is an orchard invisible."

Taught Through Trouble

Trying to trick the tranquil time ?
Time ticks to take tactful takeoff.

-Aarohi Bhattacharya

As we conclude this book, remember that this is not the end of the journey. To learn how to deal with such emotions is another skill, I hope I could convince you with the fact that such feelings exist and one must striving to learn, grow and find their purpose of living.

EVERY ENDING IS NOTHING BUT A NEW BEGINNING !

A Note Of Gratitude To My Readers

Dear Readers,

Thank you for embarking on this journey with me.

Your time, curiosity, and engagement have brought this book to life in ways I could only dream of.

This book exists because of the love and dedication

of you and my loved ones. Hope you had a mindful time reading !

May these words stay with you, inspire you, and resonate in your heart.

With deepest gratitude,

-Aarohi Bhattacharya